I0560614

The Making of a Minister

Rev. Dennis C. Raymond

Copyright © by Dennis C. Raymond June 2025

Dedicated to those whom God used to shape my ministry.

Table of Contents:

Planting the Seed   3
On Holy Ground   7
Adjustment 101   9
Getting My Feet Wet   12
Seminary Days   16
Marriage   18
Internship   20
Expectations   24
Surprising Factors   26
Confirmation Instruction   36
Looking Back   37

Chapter One: "Planting the Seed."

For two plus years, I put in my time doing what most all Lutheran youths of Junior High age do: It was usually called, "Confirmation" or in the days of my mom and dad, it would have been called, "Reading for the Minister."

The focus was on "Luther's Small Catechism," an attempt by Martin Luther in the 16th century to summarize the faith of Lutheran Christians. For me, in those formative "Junior High years," the requirement was that you memorize the words he wrote so that they would become a summary of what matters most to you when it comes to understanding your faith.

It was a class experience for the two years on Saturday mornings when there was no school to occupy our time. Just before we were to be confirmed, a "one on one" interview with the pastor was scheduled. As you might expect, it precipitated a bit of fear in many of us. What might transpire in such a setting?

But as it was, it was nothing to worry about. My pastor even complimented me on my work as one of his students. And then came an unexpected life-changing word.

"Have you ever thought about being a pastor?"

No . . . but the thought was a bit terrifying . . . Me, getting up in front of a host of people and saying words that would carry some meaning? That would not be me! I was a man of few words as I was growing up. I would rather have had my words stay put in the quiet recesses of my mind. It was my comfort zone. It was safe. What would happen if those inner words would come out? Maybe they would sound dumb . . . or maybe they would hurt someone. It was a risk I was certainly not willing to take.

Over the years, I had been the recipient of countless sermons on Sunday mornings that were well-thought-out and well presented. I couldn't imagine my doing that! So I did what most "wordless" people do – I internalized it and tried to forget it!

My confirmation pastor however didn't give up on me. When it was time for "Youth Sunday" in our church, guess who was assigned to bring the sermon for the day?

As time went on in the next few years, he gave me opportunities to get my feet wet when he was on vacation. I found that the process was difficult and demanded a lot of time and reflection on my part.

Moreover, after one of the services I conducted, my dear 8th grade English teacher commented after the service: "You know Dennis, that was a fine sermon . . . but we need to work on your grammar."

Bless her heart for her honesty. It was certainly no new revelation to me. English was definitely not my favorite subject. I could have cared less to give much importance to proper past participles, adverbs and adjectives . . . and best of all, it served me with a legitimate excuse to forget the whole thing . . . because my grammar was awful!

A few years later, when I enrolled at my alma mater, Concordia College in Moorhead, MN, my ability (or my inability) with the English language was confirmed. I tested into what was affectionately called "Bonehead English!"

Given that reality, it was clear to me that I would focus on preparing to be an architect. That was my first love!

Having been familiarized with the building process – thanks to Hilman Rice, my 5th grade Sunday School teacher who invited me to join his construction crew. Working for him for several years during the summer months I gained a fascination and a respect for all that went into the construction of a home. For my benefit, he saw to it that I experienced every step in the process.

But I guess you would say, the pastor's words lingered in the depths of my memories – in spite of my perceived inability to wrestle with words that were appropriate and understandable.

Chapter Two: "On Holy Ground"

It happened one night before I went to bed in my Brown Hall room at Concordia. I was reading my Bible – just as I usually did at the end of the day and I happened to stumble on to Exodus 3. It included the story of the message of the Lord as he spoke to Moses out of a burning bush: *"Take off your shoes! The ground on which you are standing is holy ground."*

I was familiar with the story. I had heard it a number of times. *"I have seen the affliction of my people who are in Egypt; and have heard their cry; I know their suffering, and I have come to deliver them out of the hand of the Egyptians . . ."* And then came the real kicker: *"Come, I will send you to Pharaoh that you may bring forth my people out of Egypt."* (A rather formidable assignment, wouldn't you say?)

And not surprisingly, Moses said: "Who me?!" And it didn't take very long for him to respond. *"Oh, my Lord, I am not eloquent . . . . I am slow of speech and of tongue."* And all of a sudden, the text was not just another story from the good book, but an occasion that can best be described as a type of "Holy Ground" for yours truly!

The Scripture seems to work that way. When we think we have mastered chapter and verse, all of a sudden, it creates a "holy ground" that surrounds us and we discover that God is speaking directly to us! "Slow of speech and tongue?" What kind of talk is that? "Who is it that made your mouth? " A formidable assignment . . ? Yes, if all depends on you!" Then came the words of promise:

" I will give you the words to say!"

Or in other words: No need to sweat the small stuff! You will not be alone. Do you not remember my name? It is "Emmanuel!" "God with us!" "I have heard the cries of my people who are yearning for someone like you to bring the good news of my presence to a world that is captive to unbelief and despair. Go now, and I will be with you!"

My wordless character was turned upside down! Do I trust what He says or do I go on my merry wordless way?

It was His promise that made the difference.

"I will give you the words to say."

Chapter Three: "Adjustment 101"

The very next day, with some misgivings, I dropped my art curriculum and decided to pay closer attention to my "Bonehead English" assignments. I determined that I would graduate with a major in history and a minor in psychology.

Of course, it meant that I would have to endure a study of the Greek language since the New Testament was originally written in Greek. Moreover, it was a prerequisite to enter seminary.

If I was challenged in my English courses to determine the proper grammar, the study of the Greek language was far more formidable! It was my greatest "nightmare!"

In the first place, you had to master the Greek alphabet, starting with alpha, beta, gamma . . .

Moreover, In Ancient Greek grammar, there are seven main verb tenses in just the indicative mode: each expressing different aspects of time and action. ·

Present: Describes actions happening

now or habitual actions.

Imperfect: Describes actions that were ongoing or repeated in the past.

Future: Describes actions that will happen in the future.

Aorist: Describes a simple past action, often viewed as a completed event.

Perfect: Describes an action completed in the past that has relevance to the present. ·

Pluperfect: Describes an action that was completed before another past action. ·

Future Perfect: Describes an action that will be completed in the future, by the time another future action occurs.

In addition, our Greek professor was known for his "effectiveness." To be honest, he ran his class like a military sergeant. If he sensed that you were unprepared in your lesson for the day, he would drill you and drill you in front of the class until he had made his point. In his mind's eye, the study of Greek was to always be your first priority!

And, no kidding, his fame was noted at the seminary, where it was said that he produced the best Greek students from anywhere! How "fortunate" was I to be given such an exceptional education!

Well, to be perfectly honest, I did learn

enough to recognize the issues involved in getting an accurate translation of Scripture, but in terms of personal motivation, it was in the same category as my English classes.

Chapter Four: "Getting My Feet Wet"

In the summer months, I continued to work for my contractor family friend building homes and for two summers helping to build a new church building for our congregation. It was an enjoyable experience and I was totally wrapped up in the process, still maybe wondering if architecture might be in my future.

And then, there was a call from the president of the Lutheran Free Church in Minneapolis. He was wondering if I would be interested in serving a couple of rural congregations that at the time were without "pastoral leadership."

As soon as he mentioned them, I could picture them on the South Dakota prairies – at least one of them was just a couple miles away from my Grandma's farm in One Road Township. The number of pastors available was at a low ebb, so that there were not a lot of options open for them. As it turned out, they were actually open to a "Sem Student!"

For me, it was another opportunity to address my misgivings about myself. I was working hard at our building sites during the day. Would I have enough time and energy to offer pastoral leadership to these two congregations? At the same time, it was an answer to prayer that gave me the opportunity to experience what it would be like to serve as a "pastor." So I agreed, thinking that I would have the evenings in the week to prepare for my Sunday duties.

It wasn't long after that call that I received another call from two other country congregations who were currently without a pastor. So after working with them to establish a schedule that would enable me to meet their needs, I ended up that summer serving four country parishes. Was God trying to tell me something? Was it His doing that I was given this kind of exposure to what it would be like to assume the "pastoral role?" Knowing the kind of God I was getting to know more intimately and who was totally in touch with my misgivings . . . I could hardly on my part not take a small step of faith.

The result was a busy summer – no question there. But it also forced me to engage the Scriptures on a totally different level. They were no longer just words on a page, they were a breath of fresh air in the midst of a polluted world. They were filled with insights into how He is still working in this world – if we just open up to His Spirit's leading.

Isaiah said it well: *"For as the rain and the snow come from heaven, and return not thither but water the earth, making it bring forth and sprout, giving seed to the sower and bread to the eater . . . so shall my Word be that goes forth from my mouth; it shall not return to me empty, but it shall accomplish that which I purpose, and prosper in the thing for which I sent it." (Isaiah 55:10-11)*

All of a sudden, I was beginning to realize the value of messaging this word as best I could - giving people hope and direction and purpose in accord with their Creator, Redeemer, and Spirit.

And then, another opportunity opened up in the one congregation that was so close to my Grandma"s farm:

"We have four students who are waiting for someone to lead them through Luther's Small Catechism. Would it be possible . . ."

Again, I had no experience beyond my own involvement in the confirmation process; but somehow that was a weak argument in the face of the importance of helping those four kids wrestle with the fundamentals of their faith. *"Remember,"* Paul writes in his letter to the Philippians, *"God is at work in you, both to will and to work for His good pleasure."* (Phil. 2:13)

It was fast and intensive to confront them with all the implications of Luther's catechism in such a short time, but we managed and when the time came for them to recite memorized excerpts of his catechism, they impressed the whole congregation.

I will never forget the conversation I had with one of their parents. Two of the four were cousins and lived across the country road separating the two farms. The mother told me how her daughter went over to her cousin's farm and while he was milking cows, she had him reciting excerpts of the catechism.

Another experience with those four congregations was to eventually get to know the people and hear stories not only of what they were going through, but also of how much they appreciated what I was doing.

That's what I mean by the old adage: "Getting your feet wet!" And I am convinced that it was all a part of God's plan for me as He sought to heal my trepidations.

Chapter Five: "Seminary Days"

My formal education for ministry took place at Luther Theological Seminary in St. Paul, MN. While the thought of Graduate School was a bit intimidating, I discovered that the professors were more than professionals. They were people whom God had touched and equipped way beyond my expectations. They were, once again, people who were well grounded in the way God works and gifted in sharing how that comes about.

There were moments when they challenged my ability to understand, but that was not unusual – given the complexity of theological inquiry and trying to get into the comings and goings of God's Spirit. By the time we left, we were amazed again and again as we came to a better understanding of the depth of the nature of our God and His amazing grace in dealing with us.

Seminary was once again a source of great relationships. There were certainly a lot of issues to discuss, given the attempts to master what we heard in class. And when we had reached the pinnacle of agreement, we would go "out on the town" and experience what it had to offer in terms of entertainment.

There were four families in my case that ended up with excursions people only dreamed about - like taking a trip to Colorado to attend a theological conference at the university, as well as another trip to Canada to attend the installation of one our crew to become bishop of the Saskatchewan Synod.

Chapter Six: "Marriage"

There may be some of you who wonder about this chapter. You may be thinking: What's marriage got to do with "the making of a minister?"

On the other hand, maybe it's a great resource for actually experiencing what it means to love others, particularly those people who called you to ministry in the first place. They were members of congregations who voted for you at a special congregational meeting, including the best and the worst of them!

Likely, those of you who have a life partner are exposed on a daily basis to experience what it means to actually live with and for another – "for better for worse, for richer or poorer, in sickness and in health – to love and to cherish until death brings the relationship to a close."

We human beings are a mix of good and bad. As much as we would like us to be consistently "loving" and "lovable," . . . I know of no one who might qualify.

Marriage gives us a close-up of how we

deal with that dimension of who we are. If we are totally honest, there are times when we celebrate the opportunities to be a "loving" person; and there are times when we are embarrassed with our thoughts and actions.

I remember the time I made a four-hour journey in my 1950 Dodge in the dead of winter just to connect with my beloved. The heater in my car didn't work . . . but no matter. . . my love for her was just more important. There are times like that when love prevails.

On the other hand, numerous times my selfish side was a disappointment to her.

As I look back on the 60 plus years that we have now been married, that close relationship has been a great teacher of human relations and very instructive in the way in which I seek to live in relationship with others. To live with someone who has faithfully accepted both sides of me for that many years – is truly a miracle and a blessing!

Chapter Seven: "Internship"

The third year of instruction at the seminary sent us out into the world to experience an internship assignment and to get a handle on what it actually means to work in a parish.

My internship took my wife and me to La Crosse, Wisconsin where I learned how to pastor in an inner city setting. Granted, LaCrosse was not a megalopolis, but it certainly had a city mentality that was unique and far beyond our small town backgrounds that we brought to the assignment.

I think I was the fourth intern that the parish had experienced, so it was not a big deal as far as the congregation was concerned. I did have a chance to visit with the previous intern to get a little "hands on" advice.

One of his comments was: "Just so you know, the only place you will experience the effectiveness of the pastor's preaching will be in the seat of your pants!" Well, granted, it was true to a point. His preaching was not his long suit, but he was certainly gifted in other ways.

He had to be a great administrator to have led the congregation to build the incredible church building that we saw. It had all the things that were needed and then some: a beautiful sanctuary with a hand carved pulpit demonstrating the parable of the sower; a large and effective Schlicker pipe organ; a beautiful lounge filled with lots of comfortable places to sit and converse; a small chapel, again a large wood carved background to the altar that featured the text of Psalm 51 that was part and parcel of our offertory every Sunday: *"Create in me a clean heart, O God and renew a right spirit within me."*

Outside, another carving in the stone façade of First Corinthians 13 as well as a very thoughtful granite sculpture with the position of St. Paul lying on his back with arms and legs up in the air depicting the Lord's encounter with him on the Damascus road where he was determined to eliminate anyone who was following "the Way."

There was also a massive fellowship hall that could accommodate huge gatherings, a youth room and a fireplace room.

Our supervisor pastor certainly had a keen vision when it came to seeing that the design of the building would be first class through and through!

He did give me a pretty well-rounded feel for the usual things that pastors do: visiting the sick in the hospital; bringing communion to the aged in their homes or in nursing facilities; youth ministry, confirmation instruction.

Of all those assignments, confirmation instruction was the most challenging. It all had to do with the makeup of the classes. The 8th graders were a delight to work with; the 7th graders not so much.

There may have been some in that class who were interested in what I had to say; but there were too many who had been sent there likely against their will and who needed to advertise their rebellion in some way. It was a humbling experience to say the least.

Then again, it was a lesson in human interaction. You have to somehow reach out to their life story, even when it's contrary to your own. I simply wasn't there yet.

I also ran into that contrast when I visited with the aged. In particular, I remember an interchange I had with one lady who was showing me the socks that she had knitted for the Seaman's Mission out East – she had a sunny, positive, bright disposition. Next door was another lady who literally sat in the dark.

All the shades in her room were pulled down and the conversation was depressing. I had a lot to learn when it came to identifying with the latter.

Obviously, the "Making of a Minister" was not done yet! When you run out of the right words to say, it's not time to flounder; it's a time for prayer – when you ask God to follow through on His promise to "give you the words to say!"

Chapter Eight: "Expectations"

Some of you may remember Julie Andrews singing that introductory song in "The King and I" when it came to the challenge of knowing all his children. According to the King, he maintained that the number of his kids was "somewhere over 100." I know, it was a long time ago and some of you wouldn't know who Julie Andrews is, but her song, "Getting to Know You," still rings in my head.

In case you weren't around back then, these are some of the words sung to the children by Julie Andrews.

Getting to know you, getting to know all about you;
Getting to like you; getting to hope you like me.
Getting to know you, putting it my way, but lightly:
You are precisely, my cup of tea!
Getting to know you; getting to feel free and easy;
When I am with you; knowing just what to say.
Haven't you noticed, suddenly I'm bright and breezy
Because of all the new and beautiful things
I'm learning about you . . . day by day.

Any time you move to a new community, there is that dynamic at work. As we moved from one parish to another, I think we became more intentional about that process of "getting to know you." By the time we served our last parish, a congregation of over 2,000, we used the church lounge and invited roughly 20-25 people at a time. After sharing a bit about ourselves, we asked them what they were hoping for from their new pastor. I'm guessing that the cookies and coffee didn't hurt the event either!

Chapter Nine: Surprising Factors That Contribute To "Making of a Minister"

1. The people you serve.

When it comes to growing into what the people need as a pastor, there is no question in my mind that it is the people themselves that are some of the primary factors.

Here are some samples:

Her name was Mary.

She was one of the shut-ins that I visited on a regular basis. She was always busy knitting or creating quilts, in spite of her gnarled hands, afflicted from years of arthritis.

Beyond that, what I remember about her was what she said after I had given her holy communion. (The words still echo in my memory!)

"Break forth, my soul, with joy and say . . .
.   What wealth has come to me this day.
My Savior dwells within me now . . .
How blest am I; how good art Thou!"

And then there was Emma.

She was another senior whose life was filled with the presence of the Lord. In fact, she confided in me one day as she described an experience she had with the presence of the Lord. It was so real that she could picture her Savior sitting on the foot of her bed, granting her peace and an overwhelming joy.

* * *

Her name was Jenny.

Jenny was also up in years, but that didn't stop her from inviting us up to her upstairs apartment for a meal that she had lovingly prepared. This happened again and again. She never outlived her spirit of welcome to a couple of beginners in the faith.

* * *

And then there was John.

He was a serious, dedicated member of the congregation. His extended family had a long and faithful connection to the church. He was in sync with that dedication and was currently a member of the church council. Yet it seemed that we were for whatever reason at odds with one another and found ourselves on opposite sides of whatever we did. That was the case until one night when we found ourselves in the same car after a council meeting.

For whatever reason, we seemed to be in a different mode. We ended up sharing quite a bit of our differences; but then somehow it changed when we began sharing some of our challenges and personal needs.

Our conversations were on a different level. Somehow, we discovered that we had a lot more in common than either of us had realized. It marked a significant difference in our relationships that later blossomed into a great friendship. Did God give us the words to say? I wouldn't have been surprised.

* * *

Another experience is emblazoned on my memory . . .

She was still in her thirties . . . a victim of terminal cancer. I was called to minister to her. I can still remember the apprehension as I climbed the stairs to her bedroom.

"What should I say?" "How do I console someone who is facing such a future . . . ?

She sensed my discomfort . . . and then she said with a slight smile: "Oh . . . just read to me from 2 Corinthians 4: verse 16 and following . . ."

And I did . . . .

"So we do not lose heart. Though our outer nature is wasting away, Our inner nature is being renewed every day. For this slight momentary affliction is preparing for us an eternal weight of glory beyond all comparison,

Because we look not to the things that are seen but to the things that are unseen;

For the things that are seen are transient, but the things that are unseen are eternal.

For we know that if the earthly tent we live in is destroyed, we have a building from God, a house not made with hands, eternal in the heavens.

Here indeed we groan, and long to put on our heavenly dwelling, so that by putting it on we may not be found naked.

For while we are still in this tent, we sigh with anxiety; not that we would be unclothed, but that we would be further clothed, so that what is mortal may be swallowed up by life.

He who has prepared us for this very thing is God, who has given us the Spirit as a guarantee.

So we are always of good courage;

We know that while we are home in the body, we are away from the Lord – for we walk by faith, not by sight.

We are of good courage, and we would rather be away from the body and at home with the Lord.

So whether we are at home or away, we make it our aim to please Him." (2 Corinthians 4:16- 5:9)

And from years earlier, the promise was again confirmed: *"I will give you the words to say!"*

The People . . . the very ones you have been called to serve, and their faith – they are great factors in the "Making of a Minister!"

2. Continuing Education

As I look back in retrospect, another surprising factor in "The Making of a Minister" was something that was written in the letters of call that I received and accepted. It went something like this:

"The congregation shall provide funds for the pastor to have the opportunity to engage in 'Continuing Education.'"

The seminary experience was indeed the primary source for equipping me to be an effective servant as pastor – particularly in the realms of theology and exegesis; but there were numerous areas that were almost non-existent when it came to preparing us for ordination.

The continuing education clause in each of the congregations that I served was a significant help in the making of an effective ministry.

I would like to share three continuing education programs that were most helpful in almost every congregation I served. They included the following:

A. "The Bethel Series"

Based on what you have read so far, it should be clear concerning the impact the Scriptures can have on a person's life. Wanting to share that influence with one's parishioners is understandable. I was fortunate to be called to my first congregation where Harley Swiggum's Bible Study called "The Bethel Series" was in place. The willingness of some folks in the congregation to invest in a two-year study commitment was amazing in each succeeding congregation that I served. Moreover, after they had completed the two-year study led by the pastor, they would then be asked to teach it to small groups in their congregation who hadn't as yet been involved in the program. A huge commitment? To be sure. On the other hand, to see and experience the excitement of God's Word becoming real and alive in the lives of your parishioners was so refreshing!

As time went on, the organization that produced "the Bethel Series," developed a few other courses that we ultimately used for our adult education opportunities:

"Gems for Daily Living"

Basically, it was a course on human relationships based on the book of Proverbs in the Old Testament. Very worthwhile and again, an exposure to a part of the Old Testament that is unique and scarcely used. A surprising and useful section of the Bible.

"To Love and to Cherish"

Finally, a very practical course in the relationship between a man and a woman. It explores many of the issues that face a modern marriage.

All the above courses were a God-sent word that enabled me to be an effective and successful pastor. Granted, it consumed a lot of my time in preparing for the presentations, but well worth it in helping my parishioners to experience what the Scriptures have to say about life in all of its perplexities.

B. "Organizing Around the Great Commission"

It didn't take long in my first and second pastorate, to recognize that there is a huge gap between knowing what to do and determining how it gets done. We had no such course at the seminary to deal with this. Thus, when Donald Abdon came out with his program called, "Organizing Around the Great Commission," it didn't take me long to sign up.

One of the key statements that stuck with me was his assessment of the spiritual gift of "Administration." He spoke of it in terms of its importance when he said that "It's the delivery system that gets things done!"

So I implemented the program in the last two pastorates and was impressed with the impact it had on the members of those parishes. All of a sudden, there were more people involved in the decision-making process. Moreover, they were excited to have ownership in the accomplishments that were made.

C: "Stephen Ministry"

Like many others who had high hopes for providing pastoral care to the people in their congregation and community – that was one of the prime reasons why I felt called to pastoral ministry—to bring Christ's love to hurting people. But reality quickly sets in.

There were so many needs and only one of me, and not nearly enough hours in a day. I had a church full of needs, but at the same time, as this program suggested . . . I also had a church full of people who could help. So the solution became clear: *". . . equip the saints for the work of ministry, for building up the body of Christ"* (Ephesians 4:12 NRSV)

Stephen Ministry was developed by another Lutheran pastor, Ken Haugk – who also had a degree in psychology. His approach was to extend a call to some of the members of his congregation who were gifted with listening and caring skills as well as an empathy and a willingness to engage people experiencing life's difficulties. Then, with his theological and psychological expertise, he would seek to equip them to be as effective as God had created them to be.

Thankfully, at Faith Lutheran in Spicer, I had a partner, Clarice, who was willing to share the teaching and supervising tasks. I think we were one of the first in the nation to implement the program. It required Clarice and me to attend a two-week training session in St. Louis, Mo . . . and we were off and running.

The program was so effective that I made use of it in the remainder of the congregations I was called to serve. To date, the program has taken root in nearly 13,000 congregations.

Chapter Ten: "Confirmation Instruction"

Ever since my intern experience with attempting to communicate the basics of our Lutheran understanding of the gospel with my middle school students, I gave that task a priority on my "to do" list.

Most of the possibilities that I examined and in some cases some that I developed on my own - left a lot to be desired. One of the God-given insights that helped the process was to recognize that the kids that I was trying to reach did not grow up with just a radio. So I developed a power point presentation to illustrate what the Lutheran faith was all about. I tried to pick pictures that they could identify with. Then I challenged them to think through with me what a difference the Christian faith would make if it was an integral part of their lives. At least it got their attention and I sensed that they were with me for most of the time.

Chapter Eleven: "Looking Back"

As I reflect on these 60 some years, I tried to be as effective as I could be to share the good news of Christ's presence in our lives. It occurs to me that this God who is so continually active in our lives wants in the worst way to be more than a subject for discussion but a Spirit that resides inside of us bringing about renewal and change.

Each time we gather for worship, God is active, making his way into our "insides" speaking to us through the ears and feeding us through our mouth with the bread and wine of His presence.

Secondly, as I look back on all those years of ministry, it's very clear to me that God is always true to His promises. Ever since He had my attention through the burning bush story in Exodus, He has always been there "Giving me the words to say." When I look back at all that has transpired through the years, all I can say is: "Thanks be to God!"

And finally, at reflecting on the way God works with us, it strikes me that in this attempt at encouraging me to consider the ministry, the story begins and ends with a focus on confirmation. If you remember my presumed "deficiency" in considering the possibility of pursuing a life of ministry - was my poor grammar. As time went on and I was trying to make confirmation more effective, I moved from a focus on Luther's Small Catechism to asking each of my confirmands to present a "faith statement" to describe their relationship with God. Interestingly enough, as I reviewed them, I found myself correcting their grammar. How did that happen? Again, God knew what I needed and hence, He managed to give me a new appreciation for the gift of grammar. I have discovered that it is in fact the "delivery system" that makes "words" effective.

So again, all I can say in summary is: "Thanks be to God!

www.ingramcontent.com/pod-product-compliance
Lightning Source LLC
Chambersburg PA
CBHW071354130626
46556CB00005B/2176